DOGS

# GOLDEN RETRIEVERS

by Elizabeth Andrews

Cody Koala
An Imprint of Pop!
popbooksonline.com

# Hello! My name is Cody Koala

**This book is filled with videos, puzzles, games, and more! Scan the QR codes* while you read, or visit the website below to make this book pop.**

**popbooksonline.com/golden-ret**

*Scanning QR codes requires a web-enabled smart device with a QR code reader app and a camera.

**abdobooks.com**

Published by Pop!, a division of ABDO, PO Box 398166, Minneapolis, Minnesota 55439. 

Printed in the United States of America, North Mankato, Minnesota.

102022
012023

THIS BOOK CONTAINS RECYCLED MATERIALS

Cover Photo: Shutterstock Images
Interior Photos: Shutterstock Images; Getty Images; Kasey Rajotte
Editor: Grace Hansen
Series Designer: Colleen McLaren

**Library of Congress Control Number: 2022941105**

**Publisher's Cataloging-in-Publication Data**

Names: Andrews, Elizabeth, author.
Title: Golden retrievers / by Elizabeth Andrews
Description: Minneapolis, Minnesota : Pop!, 2023 | Series: Dogs | Includes online resources and index.
Identifiers: ISBN 9781098243203 (lib. bdg.) | ISBN 9781098243906 (ebook)
Subjects: LCSH: Golden retrievers--Juvenile literature. | Retrievers--Juvenile literature. | Sporting dogs--Juvenile literature. | Domestic Dog--Juvenile literature.
Classification: DDC 636.752--dc23

# Table of Contents

Chapter 1

# Gold Star Dog

Beautiful golden retrievers are one of the most popular dog **breeds** in the United States. With their sweet faces and personalities, it's no wonder people love them so much!

Watch a video here!

ruff
feathering
short fur
feathering

Goldens have a double coat. The outer coat is **dense** and long. The **undercoat** is thick and warm. The two layers work together to protect the dog from all weather conditions. The coat also has lovely **feathering**.

A golden retriever's coat can be wavy or straight.

Goldens are medium sized dogs. They have ears that flop forward and brown eyes.

Goldens are great swimmers. Their strong tails and **webbed** feet help them steer and swim in water.

Chapter 2

# Golden Listeners

Golden retrievers were **bred** for duck hunting. This means they are excellent swimmers. Like all good hunting dogs, goldens are easy to train and listen well to commands.

Learn more here!

Goldens have lots of energy and need daily exercise. They like to run, swim, and play with their owners and other dogs. If they don't get their energy out, they might get themselves into trouble.

Goldens can live anywhere as long as they get good exercise.

Owners should spend time training golden retrievers. Training must include lots of praise because goldens are **sensitive**. They are gentle dogs who want to please their owners.

Golden retrievers want lots of love and attention.

Chapter 3

# Dog Care

Golden retrievers are always shedding. They need to be brushed often. Goldens can have hip and heart problems. Owners should take their dogs to the vet to keep them healthy.

Explore links here!

Chapter 4

# Puppies

Golden retriever puppies are born deaf and blind. There can be anywhere from four to 12 puppies in a **litter**. At eight weeks old, they are ready for their new homes!

Complete an activity here!

Puppies can begin training right away. They are smart and learn very quickly!

Goldens should start meeting new people and other dogs at this age too.

# Making Connections

## Text-to-Self

If you had a golden retriever, what kinds of tricks would you want to teach it?

## Text-to-Text

Have you read any books about other retrieving dogs? If so, how were those dogs similar to or different from the golden retriever?

## Text-to-World

Why do you think the golden retriever is one of the most popular dogs in the United States? Explain your answer.

# Glossary

**bred** – developed to act and look a specific way, or serve a certain purpose.

**breed** – a particular type of animal.

**dense** – having parts very close together with little space between.

**feathering** – a fringe of hair on an animal's coat, especially a dog's legs.

**litter** – all puppies born at one time to a mother dog.

**sensitive** – highly aware of the attitude and feelings of others.

**webbed** – having toes connected by skin.

# Index



# Online Resources

popbooksonline.com

Thanks for reading this
Cody Koala book!

**This book is filled with videos, puzzles, games, and more! Scan the QR codes* while you read, or visit the website below to make this book pop.**

popbooksonline.com/golden-ret

*Scanning QR codes requires a web-enabled smart device with a QR code reader app and a camera.